KINGFISHER
Larousse Kingfisher Chambers Inc.
95 Madison Avenue
New York, New York 10016

First American edition 1994
2 4 6 8 10 9 7 5 3 1

LIBRARY OF CONGRESS CATALOGING-IN-PUBLICATION DATA
Chinery, Michael. 1939–
Creepy crawlies / by Michael Chinery —1st American ed.
p.   cm.—(Little library)
Includes index.
1. Insects—Juvenile literature.   2. Arthropods—Juvenile
literature   [1. Insects.   2. Arthropods.]   I. Title.   II. Series:
Little library (New York, N.Y.)
QL467.2.B48   1994
595.4—dc20   93-50177 CIP AC

Series editor: Sue Nicholson
Editors: Brigid Avison, Hazel Poole
Cover design: Terry Woodley
Design: Ben White Associates
Cover illustrations: Ian Jackson
Illustrations on pp 9, 13 & 20 by Maggie Brand
(Maggie Mundy Agency)

ISBN 1-85697-502-9

Printed in Great Britain

# Creepy Crawlies

Michael Chinery
Illustrated by Ian Jackson

Kingfisher

NEW YORK

# Contents

# The smallest animals

Worms, centipedes, spiders, and flies are just some of the hundreds of creepy crawlies that live around us. Some people call these small creatures minibeasts because many of them are very small and some can look quite scary.

Many creepy crawlies are so tiny that you can only see them . . .

. . . through a magnifying glass.

# Looking for creepies

You have to look carefully to find creepy crawlies as some of them hide during the daytime. If they don't hide, these small animals may be caught and then eaten by bigger animals such as birds.

*Spider*

*Spiders can be found among leaves and plants. Centipedes look for dark damp places to hide.*

*Centipede*

# MAKE A BUG TRAP

A bug trap will help you to catch creepy crawlies that are too tiny to pick up with your fingers.

**1** Make two holes in the lid of a small plastic container.

**2** Tape a small piece of muslin or fine cotton over one end of a flexible straw.

**4** Collect creepy crawlies by gently sucking on the straw that has the covered end. Only use the bug trap for tiny creatures. Larger ones might get stuck.

**3** Push a straw into each hole and seal the joints with modeling clay.

Remember to be kind to creepy crawlies. To them you are a giant!

# Keeping safe

Some small animals have special
ways of protecting themselves from
larger ones. The baby froghopper
makes blobs of froth to hide in.

It is hard to see the leafhopper and the grasshopper because they are green like the grass. The milkweed bug is easier to spot, but birds know that it tastes nasty and leave it alone. The bombardier beetle squirts poison at its enemies.

KEY

1 Baby froghopper
2 Leafhopper
3 Grasshopper
4 Milkweed bug
5 Ground beetle
6 Bombardier beetle

# Pond life

Many insects live near a pond
or a stream. Some even spend the
whole of their lives in the water.
Dragonflies hatch out of eggs
laid in water but leave the pond
when fully grown.

*Adult dragonfly*

When it is fully grown, the dragonfly climbs out of the water. It now has large wings and can fly away from the pond or stream.

## MAKE A DRAGONFLY

**1** Twist a blown-up balloon into three parts and tie with string. Add several layers of strips of newspaper coated in wallpaper paste.

**2** When dry, paint with bright colors.

**3** Shape the wings from some thin wire. Cover with tissue paper, and draw on the veins.

**4** Cut a table tennis ball in half to make the eyes.

**5** Glue on six pipe cleaner legs.

# Wriggly worms

Earthworms live under the ground, making tunnels by swallowing soil. The worms eat tiny bits of dead plants in the soil. The rest goes through their bodies to make the worm casts we find on the ground.

Worms often come to the surface on warm, damp nights to look for leaves to eat — they drag them into their tunnels for later. The worms keep their tail ends in the tunnels to pull themselves back if there is any danger!

This worm didn't move quickly enough — a bird has caught it!

# Busy ants

Ants live in big nests that are called colonies. Their homes are often hard to find as they are usually hidden under the ground. In each nest there is one large queen ant who lays all of the eggs. The other ants are workers. It is their job to build the nest, keep it clean, collect food, and look after the queen and her young.

Worker ant

Food

Garbage

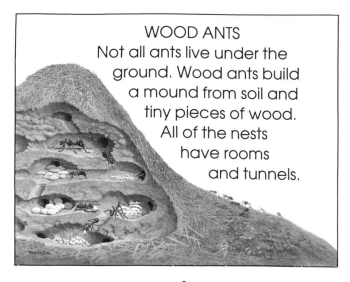

## WOOD ANTS
Not all ants live under the
ground. Wood ants build
a mound from soil and
tiny pieces of wood.
All of the nests
have rooms
and tunnels.

The workers look after the eggs and
the baby ants, called larvae.

Larvae

Eggs

Nursery

Queen

# Bees and wasps

Honeybees live together in hives. In each hive there is a queen bee and thousands of workers. Every day the queen lays hundreds of eggs in tiny wax pockets called cells. Worker bees make the cells.

These worker bees are collecting pollen and nectar from flowers to make into honey.

The queen bee lays an egg (1). After about three days, the egg hatches (2). Worker bees feed the larva with pollen and honey for nine days (3). When the larva is fully grown, the workers cover the cell with wax (4). The larva changes into a pupa (5), which turns into a new bee about ten days later (6).

WASPS
Wasps also live in nests. The adult wasps eat fruit, but the larvae are fed with small grubs.

# Butterflies

A butterfly lays its eggs on leaves. Each egg then hatches into a larva, called a caterpillar. The caterpillar eats the leaves and gets big and fat. The caterpillar then hangs upside down and turns into a pupa with a stiff, papery case.

## BUTTERFLY WINGS

Here's an easy way to make pictures of symmetrical butterfly wings.

Dip large blobs of colored paint on to one side of a piece of folded paper. Close the clean half down, smooth it gently, and carefully open it out.

Safe inside the case, the new butterfly is forming. When it is ready, it breaks out and flies away.

**6** Flying away

**3** Eating

**1** Laying an egg

**4** Pupa

**2** Egg hatching

**5** Breaking out

# Ladybugs and snails

Ladybugs are small but colorful beetles. You can easily recognize them by the black spots on their front wings. Their bright color tells birds and other animals that they will be very nasty to eat.

Gardeners like them because the ladybugs and their larvae eat the aphids that harm plants.

Snails curl up in their shells during the day. They look for food at night. Baby snails hatch from eggs.

**1** Laying eggs

**2** Eggs hatching

**3** Pupa

**4** Larvae eating aphid

**5** New ladybug

# Spiders and webs

Garden spiders spin wheel-shaped webs to trap flies and other flying insects. The webs are made from a very fine silk thread which the spider pulls out from the back of its body. Some of the thread is coated with glue and is sticky.

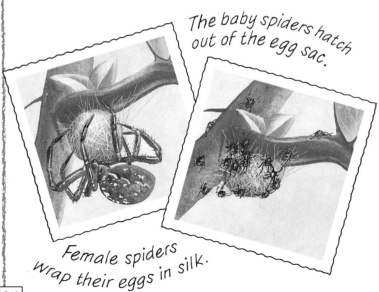

*The baby spiders hatch out of the egg sac.*

*Female spiders wrap their eggs in silk.*

The spider waits for an insect to come along and get stuck. Then it ties the insect up with more sticky thread to stop it from escaping. The spider doesn't get trapped because it walks on the spokes of the web and these aren't sticky.

# Creepies in the home

Lots of creepy crawlies live in your home, too. You may find a large house spider trapped in the bathtub. At night you may see or hear a crane fly buzzing around your room.

Blowflies come into your house to look for food to eat.

This spider needs help to climb out of the bath.

The crane fly looks like a giant mosquito—but it doesn't bite.

The blowfly mops up its food with a spongy pad around its mouth.

# Some special words

**Insect**   A minibeast with six legs, three parts to its body, and two feelers (called antennae) on its head. Most insects have wings.

Spiders are often called insects, but this is not correct. They belong to a group of animals called arachnids. These animals have eight legs.

**Larva**   A name used to describe some baby animals, mainly insects, which look very different from the adults.

# Index